D0915994

our Environment

Recycling

Eleanor J. Hall

KIDHAVEN PRESS

An imprint of Thomson Gale, a part of The Thomson Corporation

THOMSON

™

GALE

Detroit • New York • San Francisco • San Diego • New Haven, Conn.
Waterville, Maine • London • Munich

For more information, contact
KidHaven Press
27500 Drake Rd.
Farmington Hills, MI 48331-3535
Or you can visit our Internet site at http://www.gale.com

LIBRARY OF CONGRESS CATALOGING-IN-PUBLICATION DATA

Hall, Eleanor J.
  Recycling / Eleanor J. Hall.
    p. cm. — (Our environment)
Contents: What is recycling?-The challenges of recycling-The benefits of recycling-What does the future hold?
  Includes bibliographical references and index.
  ISBN 0-7377-1517-0 (alk. paper)
I. Title. II. Our environment.

Printed in the United States of America

contents

chapter one

What Is Recycling?

Since the first Earth Day was celebrated in America in 1970, **recycling** and **reusing** have become familiar words in most American households. The two words are often used to mean the same thing, but there is an important difference between them.

Reusing

People reuse their belongings in two major ways. First of all, many objects are used over and over again for their intended purposes. Examples of this are toothbrushes, clothing, pots and pans, dishes, tools, televisions, and almost every other item in one's home. Some of these items are reused for longer periods of time than others, of course, but none are discarded after only one use.

A second way in which people reuse items is for purposes other than those for which they were made. For example, an old toothbrush may become a tool to clean the tile in the shower, or a worn-out T-shirt may end up as a dust cloth. Sometimes even one-use items are reused, such as making a birdhouse from a plastic milk jug or framing a greeting card to hang on the wall.

The important thing about reusing objects or materials is that the items do not change, even

A street vendor in Senegal, Africa, displays colorful baskets made from reused aluminum cans.

though their purposes may change. The toothbrush is still a toothbrush, the T-shirt is still a T-shirt, and although it may look like a birdhouse, the plastic jug is still a plastic jug.

Recycling Is a Process

In contrast to reusing, recycling is a complicated process in which old products are changed into new ones by mechanical or chemical methods. For instance, used aluminum cans are shredded, melted, and then reformed to make new cans or other aluminum objects. Even though the end product may be more aluminum cans, the old ones must go through a complete change before becoming cans

This machine recycles plastic bottles into a cottonlike fiber that is used to make clothing and carpets.

again. Plastic soda bottles provide another example. Because there are so many kinds of **plastics**, used bottles must be carefully sorted according to their chemical type. Once the sorting is done, the bottles are cleaned thoroughly and then shredded or crushed into small pieces or pellets. This material is then changed into a thick, gooey liquid by heating it or by treating it with chemicals. This liquid plastic is formed into new bottles, or spun into fiber to make clothing and carpets.

Clearly this kind of recycling is not something that individuals can do at home. The only kind of recycling that may be accomplished at home is **composting**—turning plant waste (such as leaves, grass, or vegetable and fruit scraps) into mulch to enrich the soil. In this case, nature does the recycling with a little help from people.

Recycling is a process that breaks down products into their original materials before new products are created. Recycling requires time, money, and energy. It also requires participation by many different kinds of businesses.

Recycling Businesses

The first step in recycling is collecting and transporting recyclable objects and materials to collection centers. Local governments in many communities provide this service to citizens as part of their waste-management programs. In communities where such services are not available, private hauling companies often do this for a fee. Of course, many people transport their own materials to collection centers. Some centers are managed by local governments or by environmental groups as part of their public-service activities. Other centers are privately owned, and those who bring recyclable materials to these centers are paid market prices for them.

Several different kinds of businesses handle recyclable materials after they are collected. For instance, wastepaper (old newspapers, magazines, and office paper) is sorted into similar types and packed into bales at collection centers. The bales are then sold directly to a paper mill or sometimes to companies that buy wastepaper and resell it for processing.

From Old to New

When it reaches the mill, the old paper goes through a series of steps in which staples and other unrecyclable materials are removed. The paper is then chopped, soaked in water, and treated with chemicals to remove the ink. A thin layer of this sticky mass (called **pulp**) is dried on frames. It is then fused together between heavy rollers and wound into large rolls. The rolls are sold to companies that turn it into paper products such as kitchen towels, bathroom tissues, napkins, paper plates, and computer paper. These goods are then purchased by wholesale and retail merchants and resold to the public. In general all recyclable materials are handled in similar

These bales of wastepaper will be sold to a mill, where they will be recycled into paper products.

ways. They go from collectors to mills, to manufacturers, and finally to markets.

Another important kind of business associated with recycling is research. Research companies are constantly looking for ways to improve recycled products and reduce the costs of producing them. For instance, a group of scientists in Europe recently developed a method to blend different kinds of plastics together. This will reduce or eliminate the need to sort plastics, as well as make more kinds of plastics available for recycling. The inventors hope this process will decrease the number of plastic products that are thrown into the trash each year.

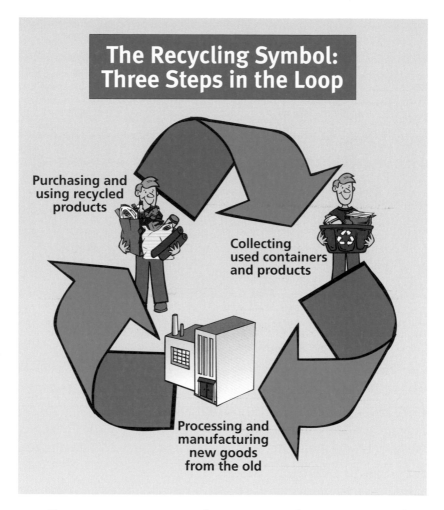

The Recycling Symbol: Three Steps in the Loop

Purchasing and using recycled products

Collecting used containers and products

Processing and manufacturing new goods from the old

Companies specializing in design are also involved in recycling. Many businesses are now producing products for which no tools or machinery existed a few years ago. New equipment was required to make such things as floor coverings from old tires, outdoor furniture from melted plastics, and new paper from old magazines and newspapers. In addition to designing tools and machinery, other companies specialize in designing new or improved recycled products.

Recycling Businesses Must Make a Profit

Once recycled goods are produced, they are advertised by marketing firms and stocked in stores. Recycled products are then purchased and used by the public. This last step, buying and using recycled products, is extremely important because recycling businesses must make a profit. The basic rule for making a profit is to sell products for more than it costs to make them. Although that may sound simple, many challenges must be met before recycling businesses can do that.

chapter two

The Challenges of Recycling

After dropping off recyclable materials at collection centers, most people give little thought to what happens to the cans, bottles, and newspapers they leave behind. What they may not know is that turning recyclable materials into new products is often a very long and costly process.

Cost Challenges

Recycling costs begin with the purchase of recyclable materials by collection center operators. Even though a lot of recyclable materials are donated, collection businesses must buy most of their waste materials at market prices. Market prices frequently change according to supply and demand. For example, when the recycling of old newspapers became popular in the 1970s and 1980s, the supply was very large.

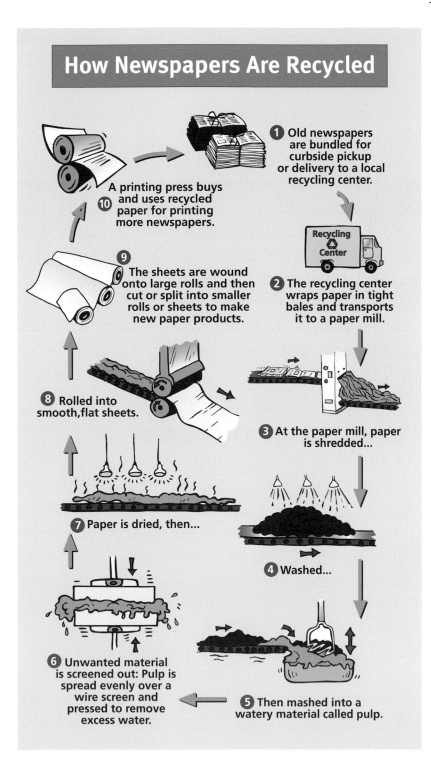

How Newspapers Are Recycled

10 A printing press buys and uses recycled paper for printing more newspapers.

1 Old newspapers are bundled for curbside pickup or delivery to a local recycling center.

9 The sheets are wound onto large rolls and then cut or split into smaller rolls or sheets to make new paper products.

2 The recycling center wraps paper in tight bales and transports it to a paper mill.

8 Rolled into smooth, flat sheets.

3 At the paper mill, paper is shredded...

7 Paper is dried, then...

4 Washed...

6 Unwanted material is screened out: Pulp is spread evenly over a wire screen and pressed to remove excess water.

5 Then mashed into a watery material called pulp.

However, the demand was low because there were not enough paper mills equipped to recycle old newspapers at that time. As a result many collection centers were stuck with worthless bales of wastepaper that they had to store or haul away at their own expense.

To encourage **conservation**, the government set up environmental regulations requiring paper mills to use a certain amount of old paper in their products. Furthermore, **consumers** began buying more recycled paper products to help conserve **natural resources**. As a result of these actions, the market price for old newspapers rose. Market changes such as these apply to all other recyclable materials as well as paper. Not knowing what market prices will be from year to year makes it difficult for recycling businesses to plan ahead.

"Uncooking" Old Tires

Another serious cost challenge for recycling industries is building and equipping new factories, or remodeling old ones. Recycling old tires provides a good example. New tires are formed by **vulcanizing** rubber, a process in which rubber and certain other materials are molded under extreme heat. Once a tire is "cooked" in this way, scientists say that recycling it is like trying to "uncook" a hardboiled egg. Because of this problem, only a fraction of the millions of tires that are thrown away in America are recycled. Those that are recycled are mainly chopped up and used as reinforcements in other products.

Many scientists today are trying to find ways of "uncooking" old tires, that is, breaking them down into their original materials such as rubber, oil, and steel. A scientist at the University of Akron in Ohio is experimenting with a sound wave machine that shatters old tires into small pieces for further processing. However, the equipment to do that costs thousands of dollars and produces only about sixty

Heavy equipment moves mountains of old tires at a recycling center in Ohio.

pounds of recycled rubber per hour. Titan Technologies Inc., an engineering company in New Mexico, developed a process that uses chemicals to break down old tires at low temperatures. Like the sound wave method, though, this new process has been held back by the high cost of building new factories or refitting old ones with the necessary equipment.

Another recycling cost is the price of energy to operate factories and machines. Recycling businesses must pay for energy sources just as families pay for electricity, gas, or oil for their homes. Prices of energy also change frequently according to supply and demand. Since it is important to conserve energy

A cleanup crew uses pellets made from recycled waste material to soak up an oil spill in Sweden.

resources as well as natural resources (such as trees and metals), difficult decisions must sometimes be made about which resources to conserve.

Waste and Pollution Challenges

Recycling produces waste and creates pollution, just as making new products does. Like all other manufacturing companies, makers of recycled products must meet health and safety standards set by the U.S. **Environmental Protection Agency (EPA)**. This usually means installing special equipment to keep harmful waste products from escaping into the air, water, and soil. As important as they are, health and safety standards do not eliminate pollution altogether. Those who oppose recycling say the damage to the environment from waste and pollution may sometimes be greater than the value of the recycled products.

For these reasons, many recycling businesses work very hard at reusing their own wastes. An example is Marcal Paper Mills of New Jersey. This company is a pioneer in wastepaper recycling. Over the years the company has not only continued to improve its recycled products, but it has created new products from its own wastes. One such new product is a pellet that soaks up spills such as oil and other liquids. These pellets are made from waste material left over from the company's papermaking process. According to a spokesperson, "The company spent six years and $20 million to research uses for the materials and build facilities to process them."[1]

Other efforts are made to reduce waste and pollution through exchange agencies operated by public and private organizations in many parts of the country. Exchange programs put companies in touch that may be able to use each other's wastes. Both hazardous and nonhazardous products are exchanged. For example, a company that uses kerosene to clean oil from its machinery cannot reuse the kerosene after oil gets into it. However, another company nearby collects the kerosene waste and uses it as a lubricant (oil) for their drilling tools. A manufacturer of steel tools in the Midwest gets its steel supply from mill on the East Coast. The fine steel dust that is created when tools are made is collected and sent back to the mill for reuse.

Marketing Challenges

The selling and buying of recycled products presents another set of challenges. Consumers (people who buy and use products) often are hesitant or unwilling to buy recycled goods for many reasons. Some people simply have little interest in buying recycled products and do not go out of their way to look for them.

On the other hand, people who want to buy recycled goods often have trouble finding them in their neighborhood stores. What they may not know is that recycled goods, or those with recycled content, do not have to be labeled that way in the United States. Many companies do it anyway to attract buyers who prefer recycled goods. Others companies do not put recycled labels on their products because of a widespread attitude that recycled goods are of low quality. While it is true that recycled goods come in different qualities, being recycled does not automatically make them inferior.

Nevertheless, this attitude can sometimes have a powerful effect on sales. "Consumers have long been trained to think of previously used stuff as inferior," writes Professor Richard C. Porter. "This training goes back centuries, to the time when recycled clothing made of recycled rags was called 'shoddy,'

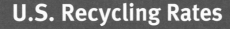

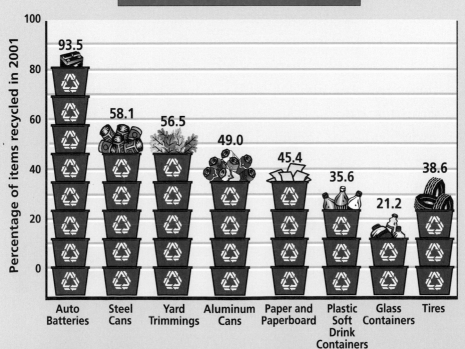

and the very word 'recycled' became a synonym for second rate."[2] A modern example comes from a company in Canada that makes ceiling tiles. Customers were pleased with the product until they learned that the tiles were made from old newspapers. When sales began to drop, company representatives stopped mentioning how the tiles were made and sales quickly went up again.

The belief that recycled goods are always more expensive than original products also has made them less popular with the public. There is some truth to this, as recyclable materials often require special machinery and more processing than new materials. For example, recycled plastic lumber (used to build decks and outdoor furnishings) is still quite a bit more expensive than wood. However, it does not have to be painted, it does not decay, and does not get eaten by termites. Also, prices are expected to drop as more people buy it and more companies start making it.

In spite of the many challenges facing them, recycling businesses and industries continue to produce goods from recycled materials. Furthermore, sales of recycled products keep on rising as better ways to make the goods are developed. Recycling has many important benefits as well as challenges.

chapter three

The Benefits of Recycling

Helping the environment is a very important reason for recycling, but that purpose does not make it profitable. It is doubtful if many recycling businesses would still be around if there were no profits to make up for the costs. Fortunately, however, many of the benefits from recycling can be measured in dollars and cents.

Reducing Landfill Costs

In the past there were very few laws about disposing of waste materials. Most of the time trash was dumped or buried in out-of-the-way places. However, as cities and towns grew larger, health and safety problems arose from such dumps and burial sites. Decaying garbage polluted groundwater and streams. It also attracted disease-spreading pests

Where Does Our Trash Go?

In one year, the U.S. generates about 229 million tons of trash. That is 4.4 pounds of trash per person per day! Where does it all go?

29.7%
Recycled
(including
composting)

55.6%
Sent to
landfills

14.7%
Incinerated

such as rodents, flies, and mosquitoes. Furthermore, dumps polluted the air with bad odors and dangerous gases. Explosions sometimes occur-red from the methane gas that is produced when garbage rots.

In response to health and safety problems, laws were passed to make waste disposal safer and more sanitary. Today waste is buried in **sanitary landfills** that are governed by strict rules. However, with the rise in population, landfills are growing in number and size. Many have had to be closed because they are full. Also, landfills are so expensive to build and maintain that users must pay high prices for dumping their wastes.

One important solution to landfill problems is to recycle many kinds of materials that were once thrown away. For instance, thousands of communities all over America no longer allow citizens to send their lawn and garden trimmings (such as leaves, grass, and tree branches) to landfills. Instead, these materials are collected separately and turned into compost to enrich the soil. Automotive recycling is another example. Instead of being junked in massive automobile "graveyards," old cars are stripped of parts that can be rebuilt and reused. Metal frames are crushed and melted to recover valuable metals. The steel industry reports that 60 million tons of steel are recycled every year, most of which comes from old automobiles.

Computer Recycling

Still another example is computer recycling. Because computers and other related electronic products go out-of-date quickly, disposal of these items has become a major problem at landfills. An even more serious problem is that hazardous substances, such as mercury, are present in many electronic products. Today many recycling companies specialize in handling outdated electronic equipment. Much of it is repaired for resale or donation. For those items that cannot be salvaged, costly metals and hazardous substances are removed and reused in the manufacture of new products. Plastic elements that can be recycled are sent to factories rather than to landfills.

Computer recyclers estimate that 150 million computers will be recycled in 2004–2005.

Recycling Conserves Natural Resources

Many of the earth's resources are nonrenewable. When the existing supply is used up, there will be no more. This is true of a number of important elements such as gold, silver, copper, iron, and aluminum. Fortunately, most nonrenewable natural resources can be recycled and used over and over again. Gold melts easily and has been recycled for

Old cars lie crushed and piled in a heap in a junkyard in the Netherlands.

thousands of years. A more recent example is the recycling of millions of aluminum cans each year.

Even renewable resources must be used conservatively. For instance, new trees can be grown, but it takes time. In the meantime recycling paper prevents overuse of existing forests. Oil is a natural substance produced from decayed plants and animals, but it takes millions of years for this to happen. Plastic is made from mixtures of chemicals and oil. Therefore, recycling plastic conserves shrinking oil supplies.

Recycling Saves Money

Both businesses and individuals may save money by buying recycled items. When recycling was just getting started on a large scale in America, recycled products were not always cheaper than new products. However, many people bought them anyway to help the environment. Over time many recycled goods have dropped in price as the sale of recycled products has increased.

Another way that recycling saves money is through **cost avoidance**. Removal of garbage is very expensive for local governments. By recycling materials that were once sent to landfills, communities cut costs and ease the burden on taxpayers. Although the recycled material itself may not bring in a large amount of money, the savings that come from avoiding the high cost of landfills is sizable. Many cities across America now save money this way. For instance, city officials in Lawrence, Kansas, reported that "A total of 6,881 tons of grass clippings and leaves, newspaper, cardboard, brushy wood waste, Christmas trees, white goods and metals, and office waste paper were recycled in 2000 for a savings in landfill costs of $135,541.35."[3]

Businesses may also avoid waste disposal costs by recycling and reusing their own wastes. Contractors building a convention center in Los Angeles, California, recycled 98 percent of the concrete, asphalt, and scrap metal from old buildings they had to demolish. They even brought machinery to the site to recycle waste materials on the spot. According to a report on the project, a great deal of money was saved, not only by reusing old materials but by not having to pay trucking or landfill fees. A bonus, of course, was keeping tons of waste out of the city's landfills.

Recycling Creates Jobs

Hundreds of recycling businesses employing thousands of workers now exist in cities all over America. In St. Louis, Missouri, a recent survey done by the University of Missouri lists fifteen hundred businesses that are engaged in recycling or in the marketing of recycled goods. These industries employ more than sixteen thousand people and bring in almost 5 billion dollars a year.

To help recycling businesses get started and succeed, the EPA operates a program called Jobs Through Recycling (JTR). Through this program, a successful recycling business was started on the Hopi Indian reservation in Arizona. Hopi residents design and make fleece clothing from recycled plastic that has been spun into thread.

Heavy equipment dumps a load of crushed green glass that will be recycled into new bottles.

Hundreds of other recycling businesses, large and small, also have been helped through grants from the JTR program. According to an EPA brochure, "The jobs created by recycling businesses draw from [all areas] of the labor market, ranging from low-skilled to highly skilled positions.

At a recycling plant in California, workers sort through paper and plastic trash in search of recyclable material.

Material sorters, dispatchers, truck drivers, brokers, sales representatives, process engineers, and chemists are just some of the people needed in the recycling industry."[4]

Some recycling companies focus on hiring people with mental or physical disabilities who might not otherwise find jobs. A computer recycling company in Baltimore, Maryland, formed a partnership with a social service agency to hire disabled workers. One of the jobs these workers do is take apart old computers and sort the parts for recycling. The president of the company is very pleased with the results and has high praise for the disabled workers.

Some Benefits Cannot Be Measured in Dollars and Cents

Although making money may be the force that keeps recycling going, it all adds up to much more than that. Many of the greatest benefits of recycling cannot be expressed in terms of dollars and cents, such as helping conserve the earth's resources for the future.

Recycling has gained a foothold in American life, but there is still much to be learned and much to be done. Whether recycling continues to succeed depends upon continued effort and cooperation among those who collect, manufacture, and buy recycled goods.

chapter Four

What Does the Future Hold?

When talking about the future of recycling environmentalists sometimes speak of "closing the loop." The loop is the familiar recycling symbol of three arrows in a circle. The arrows represent collecting, manufacturing, and buying and using recycled products. All three must work together if recycling is to be successful.

Closing the Recycling Loop

Two parts of the loop, collecting and manufacturing, have come a long way since the first Earth Day in 1970. In addition to operating recycling centers, many cities now collect recyclable materials at the curbside. Another service frequently offered by local governments is collecting yard and garden waste, making compost from it, and offering it free of charge to citizens.

Advances have occurred in manufacturing as well. There are hundreds of new recycling industries. Useful recycled products that were unheard of just a few years ago have been created. The quality of recycled products has improved over the years due to new ideas, research, and inventions.

But what has happened with buying and using recycled products? According to environmentalists, this part of the loop has lagged behind the other two. To close the loop, or make the system work at its

A resident of a Washington neighborhood hands a container full of recyclable materials to a recycling collector.

best, many more people must buy recycled goods. In fact, a slogan widely used today by recycling promoters is, "You are not really recycling if you aren't buying recycled." The responsibility for closing the loop does not fall on consumers only, however. Manufacturers must help as well. The recycled products they make must be well made, useful, and affordable so that people really want to buy them.

There is evidence that this is taking place. For instance, thousands of Web sites on the Internet offer a great variety of recycled goods for sale, both to businesses and individuals. Some of them, such as computer components and plastic pellets, are simply materials or parts that are needed to make other recycled products. Many other recycled goods offered for sale are final products. These include storage bins, carpets, furniture, building materials, playground equipment, clothing, and paper products. Many of these final products are growing in popularity.

Recycled Playground Equipment

In contrast to old playground equipment, newer types made from recycled materials are safer and much more attractive. Play Mart, a company in Kentucky, designs and makes eye-catching play areas with decks, stairs, tunnels, slides, swings, and exercise equipment. Almost everything in their playground equipment is made from plastic milk jugs. Bright colors are mixed into the plastic during manufacture so that none of the parts ever need painting. A company in Colorado, Amazing Recycled Products, also uses plastic milk jugs to make colorful sandboxes, gazebos, art easels, and other playground items.

Which Kinds of Plastics Are Recyclable?

Symbol on Container or Product	Common Uses	After Recycling, Can Become...
1 PETE	Soda and water bottles	Fiber for carpets, blankets, and stuffing for sleeping bags; also for new, nonfood PETE bottles
2 HDPE	Milk, juice, and water jugs; shampoo and laundry detergent containers	Nonfood containers or products such as motor oil bottles, trash cans, pipes, pails, and traffic cones
3 V	Vegetable oil bottles, vinyl construction materials, garden hoses, and shower curtains	Not usually accepted in home recycling programs
4 LDPE	Disposable cellophane wrap and diapers	Not usually accepted in home recycling programs
5 PP	Margarine and dairy tubs, pipes, and tubes	Auto parts, pipes, patio furniture, carpets, and toothbrushes
6 PS	Egg cartons, foam cups, and take-out food containers	License plate frames, home insulation
7 OTHER	Various bottles	Rarely recycled

A company in the Mid-Atlantic states, Recycled Surfaces Inc., specializes in creating safer and softer playground surfaces from recycled materials, mainly old tires. The surfaces are available in many colors and designs. The product is mixed into a doughlike substance and poured over an old playground. Another kind of playground surface is molded into flexible tiles that are sealed to the top of the playground. Besides being safe and attractive, these surfaces are sturdy and easy to clean.

Recycled playground equipment is rather expensive, but like other recycled plastic products, it lasts longer and requires less care. That is what the Greenleaf Elementary School in Apple Valley, Minnesota, was looking for when they decided to replace their old, outdated playground equipment with recycled, plastic units. According to the school's Web site, "The playground equipment used 21,500 plastic containers, 30,800 aluminum cans and 11,700 soup cans."[5] Raising the money for the new playground took three years. Part of the money came from a state grant. The rest was obtained from fund-raising projects in which teachers, students, and parents worked together.

Recycled Clothing from Plastic Bottles

The first plastic soda bottles appeared on the market in the 1970s. The plastic for soda bottles is made by combining oil, natural gas, and certain chemicals into thick mixtures called **resins**. The resin is then molded into bottles. When used soda bottles are recycled to make clothing, they are chopped up, melted, and the liquid is spun into **synthetic** (human-made) fibers. The fibers are woven into fabric from which articles of clothing are made. This is also the way that nylon and other synthetic fabrics are created.

Patagonia, a company that makes rugged outdoor clothing, began using fabric made from soda bottles in some of their products in 1993. Since that time, a company official reports, "We've saved some

This fuzzy fabric made from recycled soda bottles will be used to make clothing.

86 million soda bottles from the trash heap."[6] The saving doesn't stop there, however. Patagonia officials say the amount of oil saved by recycling 86 million soda bottles is enough to fill a forty-gallon gasoline tank of a sport-utility vehicle (SUV) twenty thousand times.

In addition to soda bottles, Patagonia recycles old uniforms and tents made from synthetic fabrics. Items such as these are called post-consumer stock because they are recycled after someone has used them. Patagonia also uses post-industrial stock, which is a name for waste materials from the manufacture of new or recycled goods. Both kinds of stock are wastes that ordinarily would be sent to landfills.

Ball caps, tote bags, T-shirts, and fill for sleeping bags are other products made by various companies from soda bottles. Some recycled T-shirts are made from a mixture of soda bottle fibers and scraps from cotton mills.

Recycled Paper Products

Almost everyone is familiar with recycled paper products such as paper towels, tissues, plates, cups, and writing paper. However, paper is also being recycled into some unusual materials as well. One such product is called shetkaSTONE. The name comes from its inventor, Stanley J. Shetka, a professor of art and design at Adolphus College in Minnesota. His company, All Paper Recycling Inc., mixes water and wastepaper (with some plant and cloth fibers) into a pulpy mixture that is molded into planks resembling stone. All kinds of paper are used in the process, from newspapers to glossy magazines. When dried, the planks can be sawed, sanded, glued, and nailed just like wood. The material is produced in several soft colors such as light gray, yellow, and tan. Finished products made from shetkaSTONE include table-tops, countertops, benches, chairs, and tiles.

Homosote Company also recycles wastepaper. Based in Trenton, New Jersey, this company uses

Giant bales of plastic bottles are ready to be recycled at a recycling plant in California.

about 250 tons of wastepaper each day to make a construction material. The product, called Homosote, resembles sheets of plywood and is used for inner walls and floors before the finished layers are put on. Homosote is strong, durable, and costs no more than building materials made from wood.

The Bottom Line

Although recycling is undoubtedly becoming stronger and more popular in the United States, the debate about its usefulness continues. On one hand, some people believe recycling costs more than it is worth, or they simply have no interest in it. For example, the Container Recycling Institute of America reports that over 39 billion beverage cans and bottles were thrown away in the United States in 2003. On the other side of the debate are people who want to recycle everything, but do not stop to consider the costs in money, energy, and pollution.

Between these opposing viewpoints is the position that recycling has costs as well as benefits. Many factors must be considered in deciding whether or not certain materials should be recycled. Once the decision to recycle is made, however, recycling businesses must offer goods that people want to buy, not only for the environment's sake, but also because the products are well made and affordable. Finally, consumers in great numbers must buy recycled products in order to "close the loop" and make recycling a success.

Notes

Chapter 2. The Challenges of Recycling

1. Marcal Paper Mills Inc., "About Marcal," www
.marcalpaper.com.
2. Richard C. Porter, *The Economics of Waste.* Washington, DC: RFF, 2002, p. 184.

Chapter 3. The Benefits of Recycling

3. Lawrence Waste Reduction and Recycling, "Residential Recycling," 2004. www.lawrence recycles.org.
4. Environmental Protection Agency, "Jobs Through Recycling," www.epa.gov/jtr.

Chapter 4. What Does the Future Hold?

5. Greenleaf Elementary School, "About Greenleaf Elementary," www.isd196.k12.mn.us/Schools/gl.
6. Patagonia, "Enviro Action PCR," www.patagonia .com.

Glossary

composting: Heaping plant materials (leaves, grass, weeds, wood chips, or vegetable and fruit scraps) together and allowing them to decay.

conservation: Managing the earth's resources so that both renewable and nonrenewable resources are not wasted.

consumers: People who buy and use products and energy sources.

cost avoidance: Recycling waste materials to avoid paying the high cost of landfilling them.

Environmental Protection Agency (EPA): An agency of the federal government whose mission is to protect human health and to safeguard the natural environment—air, water, and land—upon which life depends.

natural resources: Plants, minerals, metals, water, oil, gas, and any other material supplied by nature on which human beings rely.

plastics: Materials created by humans from oil, natural gas, and certain chemicals. Many different kinds of plastic materials are made depending upon the ingredients used to manufacture them.

pulp: A mixture of wastepaper, water, and chemicals from which recycled paper is made.

recycling: A process through which waste materials are changed into new products.

resin: A basic plastic material made from oil products and chemicals. Synthetic fabrics and other plastic products are made from resins.

reusing: Using materials and products over again. Items may be reused for their original purpose or for completely different purposes. In contrast to recycling, reusing does not change the makeup of the items.

sanitary landfills: Waste dumping areas that are constructed and maintained according to strict guidelines set down by the Environmental Protection Agency (EPA).

synthetic: Materials that are made in laboratories and factories rather than by natural processes.

vulcanizing: The process by which rubber and other materials are made into tires. High heat applied to the rubber mixture "cooks" the tires, thus making the recycling of old tires very difficult.

For Further Exploration

Books

Joyce Slaton Mitchell, *Crashed, Smashed, and Mashed: A Trip to Junkyard Heaven.* Berkeley, CA: Tricycle, 2001. Through photographs and text, readers take a field trip through an automobile junkyard where old and wrecked cars get smashed, mashed, and recycled into new products.

Rachael Paulson, *Sir Johnny's Recycling Adventure.* Sparta, NJ: Crestmont, 1999. Lessons about recycling and reusing are presented through a fictional story. The book also includes recycling projects for students.

Samuel G. Woods, *Recycled Paper: From Start to Finish.* San Diego, CA: Blackbirch, 2000. Paper recycling is described step-by-step in an attractive format and age-appropriate vocabulary.

Web Sites

City of Keene, New Hampshire, "Nothing to Wear? Try a Soda Bottle," (www.ci.keene.nh.us). This site contains a short but interesting discussion of how plastic bottles are produced and how they are recycled into clothing.

Consumer Reports 4 Kids (www.zillions.org). This Web site by the publishers of *Consumer Reports* magazine helps young people become more savvy consumers. Features include product- and toy-testing results, and how to avoid being misled by questionable advertising.

County of Orange, California, "Landfill Information," (www.oclandfills.com). Contrasting old dumping grounds with modern landfills, this Web site explains the care and planning that go into today's sanitary landfills. A link takes you on a photographic tour of a landfill, and another link shows diagrams of how a landfill is constructed.

Earth Odyssey, LLC, "Recycling Symbols (US)," (www.earthodyssey.com). This site discusses how the recycling symbol came about, what it means, and how it has been modified over time.

Educational in Nature, "Paper Recycling," (www .gp.com/educationalinnature/topics/recycling.html). An attractive and informative Web site from Georgia-Pacific Paper Company illustrates the steps in paper recycling.

Environmental Protection Agency, "EPA Student Center: Waste and Recycling," (www.epa .gov/students/waste.htm). Several age-graded activities about waste and recycling are offered at this site.

Green Valley Disposal Inc., "Green Valley Recycling Coloring Book for Kids," (www.greenvalley

.com/coloring/colorme2.html). Five printable line drawings about recycling waste materials at home are presented for students to download and color.

Paleontological Research Institution, "From the Ground Up: The World of Oil," (www .priweb.org). This is an excellent site for learning about all aspects of oil and natural gas—its origin, history, chemical makeup, and uses. The text is written in an easy-to-read style.

Plastic Recycling Machinery, "How to Make Plastic Wood," (www.machinerydata.com/How ToMakePlasticWood.htm). The process of making plastic wood is briefly discussed on this Web site. A bonus feature is a number of pictures of the complex machinery used to produce plastic lumber.

Thomas Recycling Companies, "Thomas Recycling's Kids' Page," (www.thomasrecycling.com /main.html). This Web site presents interesting facts and figures about all kinds of recyclable materials, including descriptions of recycling processes. Sources from which the information came are also included.

Washington State Department of Ecology: Solid Waste, "Kids Page," (www.ecy.wa.gov/programs /swfa/kidspage). A colorful, interactive Web site with information about recycling paper, glass, steel, and aluminum. Games and other related activities about recycling are included.

Index

Picture credits

About the Author

Eleanor J. Hall has long been interested in environmental concerns, having worked for the National Park Service for many years in different places and capacities. More recently she completed a teacher's curriculum guide on air pollution for the U.S. Environmental Protection Agency. Hall's other publications on environmental subjects are *Garbage* for Lucent Books and *Polar Bears* and *Grizzly Bears* for KidHaven Press. A former college instructor in social science, Hall has also written on social and cultural themes for Lucent Books. These titles include *The Lewis and Clark Expedition, Life Among the Samurai, Ancient Chinese Dynasties,* and *Life Among the Aztec.*